STABLES

Majestic Spaces for Horses

STABLES

Majestic Spaces for Horses

Olga Prud'homme Farges
Alice Vayron de la Moureyre
Gabriele Boiselle

Preface by Jean-Louis Gouraud

RIZZOLI
NEW YORK

PREFACE

JEAN-LOUIS GOURAUD

For his gods, man has built temples and cathedrals. For his kings, palaces. For one animal—and one animal only—man has built a magnificent and sumptuous shelter: the stable.

Stables are so extraordinary that even thousands of years after they were built, traces remain, even if only in memory.

The Bible mentions the stables that King Solomon in his great wisdom built to house his "forty thousand carriage horses and twelve thousand saddle horses."

Hercules redirected a river to clean out the stables of the Argonaut Augias, which is some indication of their vast proportions.

Caligula, ruler of Rome, had a marble stable built for his favorite horse, Incitatus. According to legend, Caligula gave him an ivory feeding trough, crimson blankets, and a collar decorated with pearls from the Orient."

Dictators, tyrants, and despots apparently often honor their horses by installing them in prestigious residencies (the term is entirely apt: install means, quite literally, to put in a stall).

In composing this book, Olga and Alice have revealed their most precious discoveries in conjunction with a third accomplice, the renowned photographer Gabriele Boiselle, who has also explored the many aspects of the world of horses.

So as to avoid presenting a mere repertoire, a meticulous inventory of all those fine places man has created to house and honor his horses, and to avoid turning their research into an erudite and ultimately boring encyclopedia of equestrian architecture, they had to be selective. From the tens of stables, stud farms, clubs, academies, and hippodromes that they identified, they chose the thirteen that they felt were most representative.

In this new atlas of the world, Alice, Olga, and Gabriele sought to maintain a certain geographic equilibrium: the smaller half from old Europe, the larger half from elsewhere (three in the Americas, three in Asia). They also looked for a balanced spread across history so that ancient buildings and contemporary creations are represented equally. But I believe something more lies behind these admirable, apparently objective, distribution concerns: obsessions, infatuations—or, to use an even more cavalier expression, fads.

How easily we understand them! How could anyone fail to succumb, for example, to the charm of Madame de Pauw's lodgings for her horses. Is it a stable or is it a gallery? It's certainly difficult to say, when the works of art are on the walls as much as in the boxes. In every instance for each of the buildings described and pictured in this work—be they royal stables, equestrian palaces, or temples—their construction is always born of a love story.

Out of all these remarkable stories, perhaps my favorite is the Prince de Condé who, convinced as he was that after his human life he would be reincarnated as a horse, had the stables built at Chantilly with a view to his pleasure during his future life as a horse.

Jean-Louis Gouraud

Jean-Louis Gouraud, a great rider, has written numerous articles, novels, performance pieces, and anthologies, all of which glorify horse racing. He wrote horse trainer Bartabas and wrote the text in a book titled Chevaux *by Yann Arthus-Bertrand, published by Artisan.*

CONTENTS

PRIVATE ESTATES

MASTERPIECES FOR
MADAME DE PAUW'S HORSES Louvranges, Belgium

THE FIRST TIME VISITORS ENTER THE GATES of Louvranges Estate, they find themselves following a seemingly endless winding driveway. It twists around giant horse chestnuts, lulled by the soft murmur of a hidden waterfall, goes past an avenue of lime trees, then past the monumental sculpture of an iron Don Quixote astride his emaciated Rosinante, covered with arrows, and nonchalantly comes across a green outdoor theater with carefully trimmed terraces. Between two high hedge walls, on their right, visitors catch sight of a dressage pit covered with immaculate sand, and as they continue toward the first painted wooden building, this massive white shape is entirely unexpected in the verdant universe in which it stands. Slightly stunned from this succession of sights, the relieved visitors know then that they are nearing their destination. They are struck by the refinement of the buildings and the extreme care with which each detail has been thought out. Louvranges is like a hidden casket, a work of art designed for the sole enjoyment of the horses and their bold owner.

Louvranges Estate is the convergence of four utopians in search of a playground where they can give free reign to their creative dreams. It is the culmination of four brilliant players: Mr. de Pauw, his wife Decia, architect René Stapels, and landscape artist, Jacques Wirtz.

Mr. de Pauw plays the role of the wealthy aesthete and art collector. In the mid-1970s, he decided to give Decia the buildings she needed for her riding. This project reflected her new-found passion, since for several years she had been haunting the competitive fields and holding the highest positions in European dressage.

Previous page: A horse-shaped dressage marker on a copper plaque in the riding ring.

Left: A collection of spurs from all over the world; many prestigious prizes won by the owner are displayed in the tack room next to the stable.

Right: Extreme refinement: the arm bands show not only the estate colors, but are also embroidered with their owner's initials.

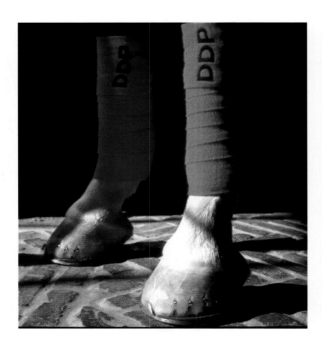

Architect René Stapels' greatest accomplishment: the Louvranges Estate riding arena, where Decia de Pauw trains her horses every day.

16

The Louis II of Bavaria dining room looks out onto the dressage pit; a sophisticated electronic system allows the glass walls to disappear completely into the ground.

Decia de Pauw leads her horse toward
the stable after a work session in the
dressage pit.

The saddle room is the center of the house, leading to the riding ring, stables, tack room, dining room, office, and residency rooms, as well as the garden. Here, horses and guests alike admire the paintings of the masters.

Their friend René Stapels was entrusted with the design of the equestrian buildings surrounding the house. Stapels, who was more familiar with the design of office buildings (he was the architect for the World Trade Center in Brussels), listened closely to their requests. Decia de Pauw's directions were crystal clear: the building should bring together the stables and the riding ring in an organic whole, inspired by the great Kentucky farms, specifically Calumet Farm.

The result is extremely surprising: the different buildings appear to be spread all over the property, yet they are closely connected. The facades are covered with bright white shutters, and the wooden support beams are painted a carmine red that borders on deep bordeaux. This striking American reference is all the more surprising in the heart of Belgian Wallonia in that the Calumet Farm model is set in great open meadows. Here, on the other hand, the garden circles the house closely, and sometimes even seems to enter it through large bay windows that disappear by dropping down into the ground.

The stables form the ground floor of the main building. There is nothing particularly revolutionary about their design since, very sensibly, Stapels did not wish to "transform the way of life of horses with architectural daring." On the contrary, he confides, "it was all about adapting the buildings to the needs of the horses." Hence, the six generously sized stalls are arranged around a wide central corridor.

Stapels has a deep respect for stable building materials: bubinga wood, with its deep walnut color, lasts for years and resists the kicks of the strong young stallions. On the wall, sober, varnished white tiling adds to the stables' impeccable appearance. Small rectangular bricks, fitted together in chevrons, cover the floor with an old patina. Traditionally made following a local method, they accompany the horses' footsteps with a hollow and melodious sound all over the ground floor of the house, creating an elegant cohesiveness among the stables, saddle room, and adjoining rooms. Between each of these rooms, heavy bubinga doors swing silently.

Once harnessed in the saddle room, which also serves as the entrance to Decia's house, the horses are taken to the outside dressage pit or the riding ring, Stapels' great achievement at Louvranges. This riding ring was built at the same time as the stables, although its aerial architecture is entirely different. Under a vault that is reminiscent of the upturned frame of Noah's ark, large windows filter the park's luxurious greenery. The curved lines of the frame stand out like accolades against the white of the rest of the building. A small square lantern, topped with a weathervane in the shape of a horse, anchors the building to the lineage of big American horse farms.

The great originality of the present site, and of the architect's stroke of genius, is that the stables are part of Decia's home: she sees her horses, at work or in their stalls, from every point in the house. At Louvranges, everything is organized around the lives of the horses: the entrance to the stables is also the ante-chamber for Decia's visitors; the saddle room serves as the entrance hall to the house; the walls of the living room and the library of the residence have bay windows overlooking the riding ring; while the dining room, in the style of Louis de Bavière, looks onto the dressage pit. This promiscuity is all the more surprising in that these rooms, shared by humans and horses, are filled with exceptional works of art: Renaissance buffets, terracotta Han horses, bronze Burmese lions, and contemporary paintings, including an Andy Warhol triptych of Decia de Pauw in her riding kit.

This mixture of genres is also found outside the house: the park is a work of art, designed and created by a nurseryman-poet. Jacques Wirtz, who created the Tuileries gardens, as well as the gardens of the Elysée Palace and the park at Chaumont-sur-Loire, to mention just a few, envisaged a veritable vegetal architecture around the stables. Wirtz sees gardens as houses: he arranges rooms in them, each one different and with a specific function. The park at Louvranges Estate is enclosed by many hedges that determine what you look at and where you walk.

Decia de Pauw somewhat mischievously assures visitors that her horses "are used to strolling among ancient and modern sculptures. They contemplate the works of art and delight in the gentle ambiance of classical music."

The race champions are music lovers: in their stables, opera music accompanies their daily life.

OPEN STABLE El Atalaya, Argentina

SOME OPEN SPACES CALL YOU TO CROSS THEM, and then call you to stay once there. El Atalaya is just such a place. Not far from Buenos Aires, in a garden of delights, the horses enchant the landscape and stables that have adopted them. Nature rules sovereign at El Atalaya. The stables sit in an endless plain that often echoes with the pounding of hooves. The space is defined only by the green of the grass and the blue of the sky. The stables open immediately onto the exterior, allowing the outside to permeate the inside. The horses thrive on the fresh air that breezes through the stable, nurtured by a universe of exquisite refinement.

The patron of this haven of peace, Count Federico Zichy-Thyssen, is passionately dedicated to his Arab thoroughbreds, and in the small estancia their well-being is clearly his top priority. "I am but a guest here," he is fond of saying. A guest so in love with his horses that he built a living room in the middle of the lavish stables! Here, under the bright eyes of these sons of the desert, the Count receives his friends.

Architect Fernando Bustillo, who created the stables, took his inspiration from early Spanish culture. He was loyal to the canons of the Jesuits who came over from the Old World some four hundred years ago: columns and cloisters, ironwork, moldings, and tiled roofs . . . these are all references to the models the first missionaries brought when they settled in the New World.

The Count's residency looks over the main stable. From the covered way running along the gallery, Federico Zichy-Thyssen can watch over his thoroughbreds. Here he too enjoys the open space where his horses, even while they are in contact with humans, live serenely, without feeling imprisoned.

Previous page: Not far from Buenos Aires are the El Atalaya stables: at 15,000 square feet, they are a temple to the glory of Arab thoroughbreds. The stables came of the encounter between their patron, horse enthusiast Count Federico Zichy-Thyssen, and architect Fernando Bustillo. Today El Atalaya is the largest stud in South America.

Opposite: The atmosphere in the stables is fresh and luminous; the architect achieved this effect by allowing the central walkway to open directly onto the exterior at either end and by installing light shafts in the ceiling, through which the sunlight pours. Horses are more sensitive to heat than to cold; it is important, therefore, to keep them cool, in the most natural way possible.

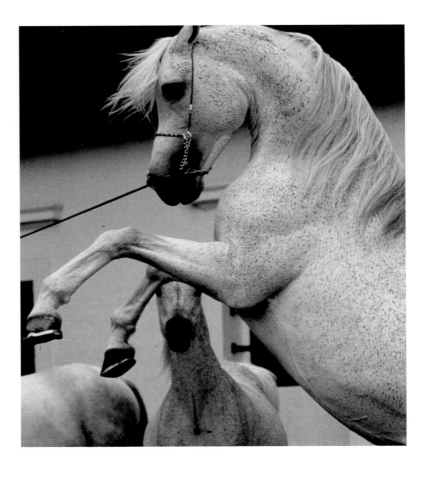

Previous page: In 1989, Count Zichy-Thyssen fell in love with an old barn and its surrounding landscape and decided to turn it into a stable for his stallions. He bought the 1,000-hectare estate and dedicated it to the breeding of Arab horses, as well as to farming.

Opposite and below: Today there are 130 fillies on the stud farm, in addition to show horses and horses that work on the estancia; all in all, nearly 300 horses. Many of the most successful stallions in the stud are originally Egyptian; for instance, El Shaklan and Anaza el Farid.

Following page: The arcades of the main stable, with its whitewashed walls, columns, ironwork, brick pavement, and roof tiles, all point to architect Fernando Bustillo's source of inspiration: the architectural models of 400 years ago, imported from the Old World by Jesuits.

Breath inspires every moment of the day: the breath of the stones, the fluidity of the buildings, and the circulation of light. "The stable is wide open on all sides, and I was free to play with the air as I thought best, creating a fresh and luminous ambiance. I had only to ensure that there were no drafts, which are harmful for horses," explains Don Bustillo. The central walkway, which opens to the outside at either end, allows the breeze to flow through, keeping the stables cool. In a breach of Spanish Jesuit architecture, the stables are filled with daylight: pools of light flood the main gallery, whose white chalk walls radiate their luminosity all day long. The architect, who wanted nature to express itself, specifically sought this natural lighting. "The inspiration lies in a place even before you touch it. The creation is already there in nature, and each space calls for an appropriate response. The challenge is to find it and foster it, so that our creativity can emerge. The combination of feelings, imagination, and technical know-how leads to perfection."

The arcades of the galleries lining the inner courtyards and the main stable are also strongly influenced by Spanish Jesuit architecture. Here we find peaceful cloisters with arches resting on whitewashed brick pillars. They add to the charm of the buildings while improving air circulation. More importantly, they keep the stalls in the shade. The other buildings, which are smaller and less

From inspiration to harmony: according to Fernando Bustillo, El Atalaya's architect, a combination of feeling, imagination, and technical know-how must come together to produce perfection. Here, a covered way offers a viewpoint from which to admire the horses in the main stable. The floor, made of a circular arrangement of bricks, is inspired by the paving of a Florentine palace.

elaborate, also refer to southern European architectural canons: ascetic, whitewashed walls, tiled roofs, and the stocky silhouette of solid rural country houses. But the buildings are not all the same, for when Don Zichy-Thyssen bought the land in 1989, he fell in love with a charming old barn that already stood there, which he turned into the stallions' stable. Its style is somewhat crude, but the proportions and space matched the Count's vision exactly.

In the early morning, after their first maté, the grooms leave for the stables with firm steps. The precious horses dance to the calls of the herdsmen. The men hang their felt hats on wooden knobs on either side of the stable doors. These knobs run all along the stalls and are made of a very strong wood that the horses can teethe on as much as they like without hurting themselves. These knobs are also used to hang up Don Zichy-Thyssen's luxurious silver encrusted harnesses.

After their morning cavalcades, the thoroughbreds return to their stalls. The sounds of horse feet echo throughout the main gallery. Here again the horses' comfort guided the design of the building in curved lower walls. These curves were studied, designed, and requested by Don Zichy-Thyssen to allow the horses to lean against the walls without the risk of misshaping their limbs, which would alter their sense of balance. As a breeder who hopes to refine the ideal Arab horse, he wants to avoid this risk at all costs. The horses bred at El Atalaya have been very successful in South America and beyond.

The stables are built primarily from traditional materials: the paneling is metal sheathed with wood, like the traditional walls built for the Basque game of pelota. The iron is invisible, and hence unobtrusive, but it makes the doors extremely strong. The floor is paved with the type of bricks the Jesuits used for road surfaces, laid sideways, rather than on the flat. The aesthetic of the pavement is Italian; in fact, the circular arrangement of the floor of the hall, in which central nerves link the pillars to the colonnade, is inspired by the paving of a Florentine palace.

El Atalaya is all about simple but careful luxury for the most beautiful horses in South America . . . luxury as gentle as a breeze.

A true stable master, Count Federico Zichy-Thyssen decides on the crossbreeding and lineages, and selects horses to represent El Atalaya in international shows. He has given these horses a sumptuous stable that seems sheltered from the passing of time.

HIS MAJESTY THE KING'S
STUD FARM Bouznika, Morocco

EVERYTHING ABOUT BOUZNIKA IS GRAND—the stables, the paddocks with thick green grass, the luxurious, yet functional, buildings, and the herd of 150 individually selected horses. Bouznika was designed by an equestrian king, his late Majesty Hassan II, to reflect the prestige and glory of the most famous Arab thoroughbreds.

To discover one of the most beautiful stud farms in the world, one must understand the motives of its creator. Half way between Casablanca, the economic capital of Morocco, and Rabat, the administrative capital, the geographical position of this stud ensures that its royal owner is never too far from state business. To find eternally green pastures, you need a constant water supply, found here in the nearby wadi river valley, supplemented by a system of dams. This ideal site offers a temperate climate that ensures that the horses are spared the heavy summer heat. In Morocco, of course, this implies that we are near the Atlantic.

Put all these directions together and you arrive at Bouznika, a small town in a verdant, luxurious, and harmonious setting, where royal horses frolic in the fields. After the sumptuous drive, lined with palm trees and bougainvilleas, that leads up to the stud farm's main gate, and judging from the grandeur and archetypically Moroccan beauty of the domain entrance, it is easy to imagine that the king of Morocco's stud farm has been here, sitting on this soft hillock, with the stream flowing below in the wadi, for centuries. Yet this monumental building was in fact built from scratch, at an incredible speed, in 1986. That was the year that His Majesty Mohammed VI, then Crown Prince, hosted the World Arabian Horse Organization (WAHO) conference, at

Left and page 38: The entrance used by employees every day. His Majesty arrives on the main driveway, passing through the paddocks that face the palace (next page). Both entrances impress visitors with their vast horizons.

Opposite: Following the tradition of the Alaouite dynasty, His Majesty the King rides to prayer on horseback during religious festivals.

Bouznika is a palace, a stable, and a stud farm famous for the Arab horses it breeds, but it is also a private golf course, built for the leisure of the royal family members and their friends.

The estate is totally protected from outside eyes, like a jewel in its verdant case. Below, the stable for Barbary horses, built shortly after the Arab horse stable, but in the same spirit and style.

which some sixty nations are represented by 400 individuals, each ready to do virtually anything for Arab thoroughbreds. In the light of such prestige and deeply felt passions, the king decided to create a great royal stud farm worthy of Arab horses and the Moroccan colors specific to their breeding. The farm's design was entrusted to an architectural celebrity in the international horse circuit, Amid Abdelhamid.

Indigenous craftsmen worked together to create a true palace. Arcades of stone lacework, hand-painted wooden doors, stalls fronted by wrought iron gates, pillars with finely sculpted capitals, fountains, candelabra, pools, flower beds . . . Every paddock is surrounded by fences painted white and ocher, with a gate bearing the stud farm's logo: the silhouette of an Arab horse beneath a crown.

Everything at Bouznika is symmetrical, balanced, and exceptionally well-maintained. A veritable squadron of stable hands, all wearing red and white, care for the farm, polishing, sweeping, and dusting every hidden corner.

To visit Bouznika is not so much to explore the pathways of a stable as to enter the labyrinth of a palace,

Right: Every door is hand-painted in red and gold lacquer, with traditional geometrical motifs. On the right of each stall, a small wooden frame gives the horse's name and pedigree.

Below: Flowers, and zelliges, small mosaic enameled ceramic pieces, decorate the pillars; stone lacework arcades; the country's natural colors; its pace and rhythm . . . Every decorative aspect inspires a sense of balance, charm, and a certain royal rigor.

Each stable bay ends with a small, purely decorative kiosk. Right: the magnificent Imperial Mashhar is the most prestigious thoroughbred stallion in His Majesty Mohammed VI's stud farm.

even if this seems incompatible with the everyday existence of 150 horses that need to be fed, watered, currycombed, and exercised in the paddocks. In fact, as in all palaces, there is a front stage, where the royal family and its visitors parade, and then there is the other world, in the wings, where the daily stable activities take place.

On the stage side, the residents leave only for the display paddocks, and are always shown in their best light. In the wings, the horses are fed, watered, and cared for … all through the stall's back door.

Two large, almost identical buildings, one of which is reserved for Arab thoroughbreds and the other for Barbary horses, function in exactly the same way, with flawless organization. To complete this arrangement, behind high walls a "third" stable was added, to shelter the horse training and the storage of straw, barley, etc.

Whether it appears as a historical monument or a palace, the stud farm of His Royal Majesty the King, certainly deserves its name. This is a breeding farm, with about fifty carefully selected brood mares and superb stallions, including Imperial Mashhar, an incredible Arab horse, black as ebony, which was world champion in 1993. This spirit of enduring quality is thanks to His Majesty the King Mohammed VI: the royal will ensured rigorous choices of exceptional Arab horses, throughout the world and especially in the United States, in order to constantly improve the breeds at Bouznika.

Today Bouznika is known throughout the world for the purity and beauty of its horses, as well as for the incomparable delights of the stud.

Previous pages: Behind the carved cedar door is an entrance hall, covered with paneling and zelliges. It leads to the trophy room, where the prizes won by his Majesty's horses are displayed, as well as gifts presented to him, such as saddles and sculptures.

Opposite: All the stalls look onto the center of the palace, so that each horse may be admired. But there is always a second door, toward the back of the stables, for the stable hands to care for the horses.

THE PINK STABLES OF LUIS BARRAGÁN

Cuadra San Cristóbal, Mexico

TWO WALLS, THAT'S IT. SO PERFECTLY SIMPLE. In the stables Luis Barragán designed at San Cristóbal, in the Mexico City suburbs, all his art is condensed in just two walls; that's all it took for the expression of this architectural genius.

Barragán's universe throbs with vibrant colors: the boldest shades come head to head, rub shoulders, and echo one another. Barragán's walls are pink. Salmon pink, hot pink, artificial strawberry ice cream pink, pale pink burnt by the noonday sun, or pink like lips. Always pink, pink as is rarely seen across entire walls.

That's all very well, but what about the stables? Two walls, however pink, have never sufficed to shelter horses. The fact is, visitors leaving San Cristóbal will find it hard to recover their senses. Still drunk on the space and brilliant hues that have seared their minds, they will find it impossible to describe objectively what they have seen. At most they might express the sense of plenitude that settles in them in the courtyard of San Cristóbal.

Very few contemporary architects have engaged in the exercise of designing stables. In 1966 at San Cristóbal, Luis Barragán adeptly skirted around the question of how to build a "house for horses" and instead structured space itself: he modeled perspectives, imaginary lines, basic shapes, and full planes of flat color. Drawn up with a most attentive eye for unusual detail, the architecture of the San Cristóbal stables is nevertheless disarmingly simple: a square courtyard defined by two colored walls, a row of stalls and an end wall that leads to a fountain. It is a homogenous spatial whole in which the conception of space is almost vertiginous: when a horse enters this stage, it seems to glide across the floor.

Left and page 54: Out of the arid ground, just outside of Mexico City, arose casa San Cristóbal, the work of Luis Barragán. A keen admirer of horses, he created for them a space built of shadows and colors.

Right: Harmony hanging by a thread: three times over, Luis Barragán moved the North wall before he found the ideal position with which to satisfy the request of his commissioner, Folke Egerström.

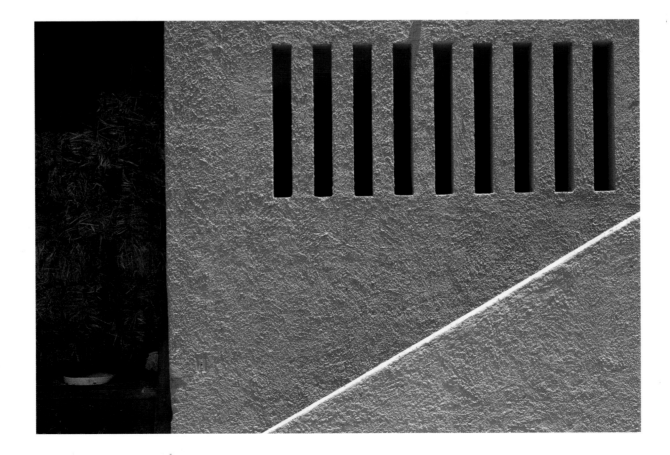

*Opposite: A wall, a tree, and a fountain
form a minimalist set originally designed
for a single actor on stage: the horse. But
occasionally the pool has other guests.*

*Following pages: Cristóbal Egerstöm,
Folke's son, is the current stable owner.
He has represented his country in the
Olympic Games in horse jumping
several times. He trains not far from his
house, at the Hípico Francès Club, which
Luis Barragán also frequented.*

Some of the architect's recurring themes: the marriage of shadow and light, the quest for the sublime.

The center of his creation, the stable
has a pool for the horses; here the
water multiplies the interplay of light
and shadow.

Let us explore the stables with those who helped Barragán create them. Andrés Casillas de Alba, Barragán's architect friend, collaborated with him for many years. He tells of Barragán's moment of hesitation when he received the commission for the stables from Folke Egerström. He remembers his uncertainty about how to arrange them as a whole. Eventually, Barragán resolved the dilemma practically: "We'll set off across the country to visit the old Mexican *haciendas* and ranches. When we find beautiful buildings, we'll measure them as we measure our paces." Out of this experience was born a curious combination of very modern architecture and local influences: two tree trunks in the center of the courtyard where the horses are tied up; an awning to protect the horses from the sun; a tree throwing a fragile shadow across the yard. These distinctly Mexican elements are all references to the architect's home country, from which the space draws its fundamental inspiration.

We can well imagine the two architects, searching out the beauty they loved, striding up and down the country, delighting in these preparatory promenades. Casillas de Alba describes Barragán's process: "Luis was fond of citing Oscar Wilde: art is the materialization of an idea. Without the idea, you have nothing but a hollow falsity. The work of the creative artist is first to find an idea; Luis' work is precisely to that. First he learns how horse baths work, then he picks up his pen and envisages one creatively."

Cristóbal Egerström, Folke's son, has a more pragmatic view of the architect's work. Cristóbal was only a few years old when his father bought the land in the Mexican suburbs and asked Barragán to build on it. The drawings and construction moved forward quickly. By the end of 1968, the stables were finished and work on the fountain had begun. But the walls, especially the longest one, apparently upset the architect's aesthetic vision. "Luis

Left and opposite: Luis Barragán rode all over the Mexican countryside with his architect friend Andrés Casillas de Alba. They sought out and studied traditional architectural features (awnings, posts for tying up horses) and their proportions, in order to integrate them into San Cristóbal.

was not satisfied with the initial position of the wall. He had it moved, but apparently it was still wrong. So he decided to move it one last time . . . my father was furious about what he saw as a useless expense, since the third version was just a foot away from the first!" Cristóbal recalls. "Yet perhaps it was quite simply moving the wall over that one foot that gives the place its marvelous balance. Wherever you stand in the courtyard, it always feels absolutely right," confides the owner of San Cristóbal. He houses his horses there and has ridden them in several Olympic Games.

Barragán has always been fascinated by the beauty of horses. Perhaps this is why the architecture of the San Cristóbal stables is the quintessence of his art. As he often said: "The design of these stables was an opportunity to bring together all the elements I had been looking for over the years: the stables, a pool, a drinking trough, a house. The entire spatial design was organized around these centers of activity. This space was truly created for horses." This is clear, for example, in the pool that gently slopes down through the courtyard for the horses to relax in after work.

The San Cristóbal stables are also harmonious because Barragán is a master of light and shadow. The building that houses the stalls, graced with an awning that throws a deep area of shade, is in marked contrast to the colorful planes of the walls. The course of the sun tips these shapes, making the colors dance.

Barragán was obsessed with beauty, static and mobile—the beauty of objects and the beauty of a scene. The pool and the fountain filling it with crystalline water were designed specifically to create such beautiful scenes. Barragán imagined the horses, excited by the splashing water pouring into the pool, glowing with a sudden beauty like Bucephalus.

In the geometric entity formed by these colored walls, the tree, sand, and water are static, natural elements. When a horse walks into this fixed, mineral set, it establishes a new scale of values, becoming a dynamic form, bringing movement into a fixed world. The culminating point in this dazzling Mexican presentation of beauty is the horse, as it finds a new form of expression, between two pink walls.

Luis Barragán is a magician of simplicity, a funambulist of perspectives, and a juggler of color. Yet his creation exudes serenity and is full of nobility.

ENTERING INTO THE CLAN, MANDERSTON HOUSE Berwickshire, Scotland

TEA ROOM

When architect John Kinross asked his sponsor, Lord James Miller, what his budget was for building a stately home and stable, he was told that his question was meaningless. All Lord Miller asked was that the architect design a unique architectural ensemble whose brilliant style would reflect its owner's wealth and his status as a country gentleman. Consequently, Kinross was able to make many of his greatest dreams a reality.

Manderston allowed Kinross to indulge his passion for the Edwardian style. As he perfected this style, he was also free to express his own inventiveness. Lord Miller did have some specific plans, however, particularly in regard to the construction of the stables. As a great hunting enthusiast, and the County Master of the Hunt, he was adamant that his horses should be housed in the best possible conditions. In Scotland, the treatment of horses is taken very seriously, particularly those that are involved in the noble art of hunting.

The stables stand at the entrance to the private Manderston Estate. At the time of their construction in 1895, the light beige sandstone they were built from and their classic Edwardian style and purpose were a magnificent reflection of the region, era, and lifestyle.

Still today, the stables are filled with the barking of the pack that follows hunting parties across fields and forests from dawn to dusk. At night, the exhausted horses and hunters return to Manderston. While the horses rest in their comfortably large stalls, the hunters gather in the

Previous page: In 1895 Lord James Miller had the stables to house his hunting horses built at the entrance to his estate. Today Manderston House belongs to his descendant, Lord Palmer.

Left: The portal to the courtyard of the Manderston House.

Opposite: Nowadays the boxes that look onto the vast square courtyard house only three horses. In days past, the local elite gathered here in the early morning before the hunting parties set off.

majestic Manderston House. All will dream of the resounding trumpets, the foxes fleeing through the woods, and the wild races through the green Scottish hills.

To cross the threshold of the Manderston property is to undertake an initiatory journey. The stables are the key to the Scottish clan. They stand just behind the imposing wrought iron gates of the estate. From the road, one sees their roof behind the endless, gray stone walls that surround Manderston House. But above all one hears the hollow sound of hooves on the granite paving of the courtyard, echoing under the entranceway.

Linear perfection, strict reserve in decorative elements, the rigor of the arches . . . the moment is solemn at Manderston, frozen in the nobility of curves and stone.

This sandstone is used for all the beautiful buildings of the Borders, on the south eastern edge of Scotland. It is a stone that is whipped by the glacial wind of the nearby North Sea, a naked, raw stone, which proudly offers its solid edge to the rain. From the outside, the Manderston stables reveal no intimacy at all; they stand in a "representative function" that is very important to the powerful clan ruling the area. As pompous as one of Elgar's cantatas, they share a classic perfection and arrogance.

Despite this, the stables Kinross designed were allowed a few decorative elements, such as the pediment and pilasters framing the entranceway. These details remind us that Kinross spent his younger years in Italy, mainly in Florence, which dazzled him. For example, there

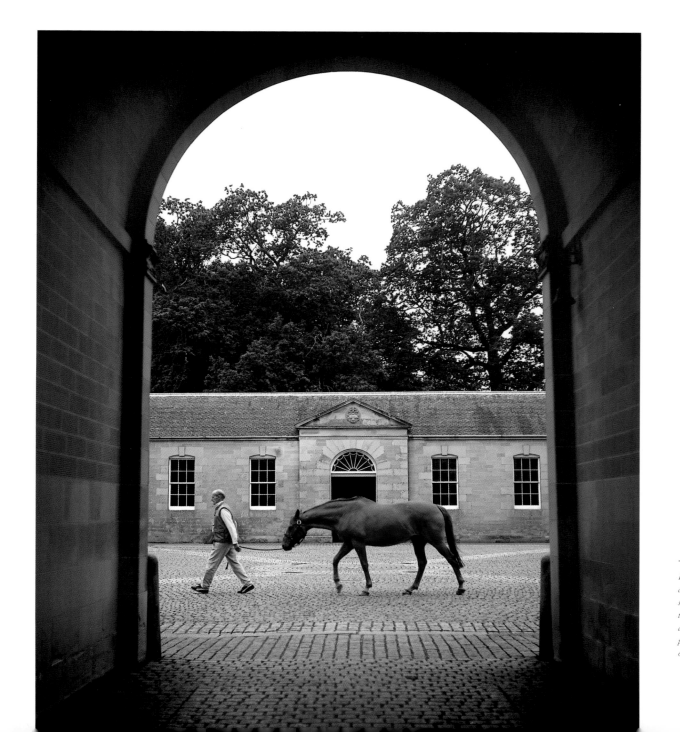

Left and right: Architect John Kinross created the stables in purest Edwardian style. The sandstone of Berwickshire, in the Scottish Borders, lends itself admirably to its sober lines. The regular paving of the courtyard emphasizes the orthodoxy of the architectural whole.

is also a bas-relief showing a hunting scene in which horses, with their bellies to the ground, chase after an animal whose ears are half rabbit, but whose bushy tail makes it half fox.

The interior of the stables provides the requisite comfort. Everything here is warm and rounded: the hard stone outside gives way to heavy mahogany paneling, the curves of the stalls follow those of the horses within, and the vault of the ceiling frame filters the icy North Sea wind, turning it into a pleasant breeze. The horses walk across the brick floor with a muffled step, while two large copper balls, decorating each stall, reflect and lengthen their golden silhouettes. At sunset, when hesitant rays of sunshine light up the rooms, gleaming colors flame, from yellow gold to glowing amber.

Are the stables the way in to the aristocratic Scottish clan? Lord Palmer, the great, great, grand nephew of the founders of the estate, who divides his time between Manderston and the House of Lords, talks about his horses with shining eyes. With rapture he describes hunting parties: the barking of the pack following the lead hound—hallowed champion several times over—the early morning gatherings in the luxurious countryside around Manderston. All of a sudden, at the signal, one is plunged into an era that is not entirely in the past nor in the world of today. Does Manderston have the power to stop time, one wonders?

In any event, the Manderston stables do not belong to the automobile era. Built in 1895, at a time when automobiles were still distant inventions, the stables lost their initial use when, ten years later, the stately home was built a hundred yards away, complete with garages for the family cars. From then on, the stables were dedicated solely to leisure.

In Berwickshire, they like to say that Lord Miller wanted to impress his wealthy family-in-law with Manderston. When he asked Kinross to build the stables at the entrance to his land, he was in fact testing the architect. But there is no doubt that the result surpassed the Scottish Lord's wildest dreams, for a few years later, he asked the same architect to undertake the construction of the main residence.

The solid silhouette of the stables stands at the entrance to the estate. Unlike the residency, a few hundred yards away, the stables are striking because of the simplicity of their lines.

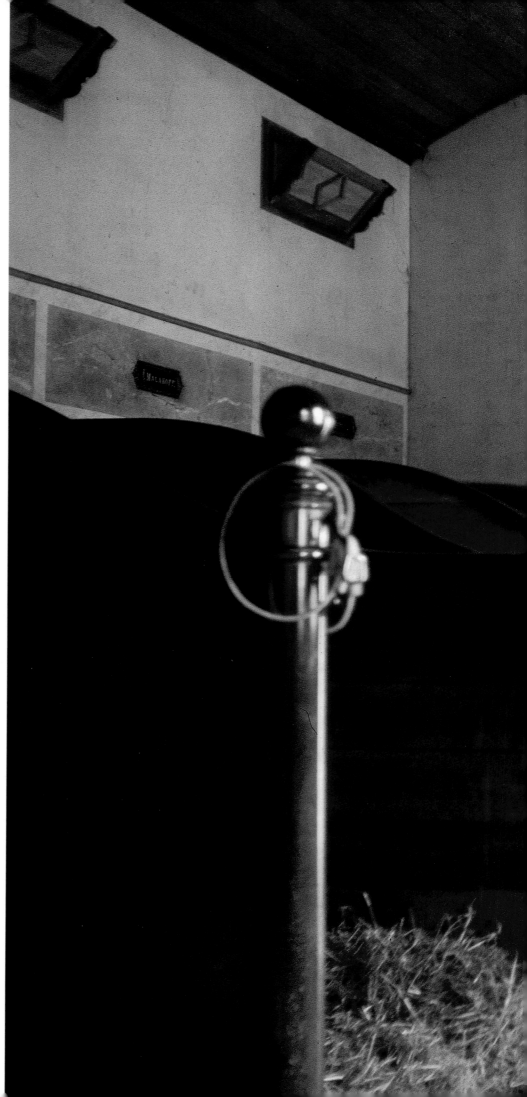

Opposite: These days the stables seem deserted, even though they still echo with their past splendor, and the barking of the impatient pack is still heard during the hunting season. Originally the boxes were reserved for saddle horses, while the stalls were for carriage horses. In the evening, these stables are flooded with warm amber rays; they offer a lifesaving shelter from the icy North Sea winds.

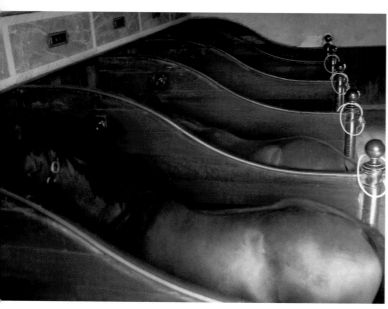

Mahogany paneling, heavy copper doorframes, marble paving on the floor, and harnesses in the Miller family colors: in the eyes of the world, the stables reflect their owner's wealth, but they also reveal the veritable passion of those who built them.

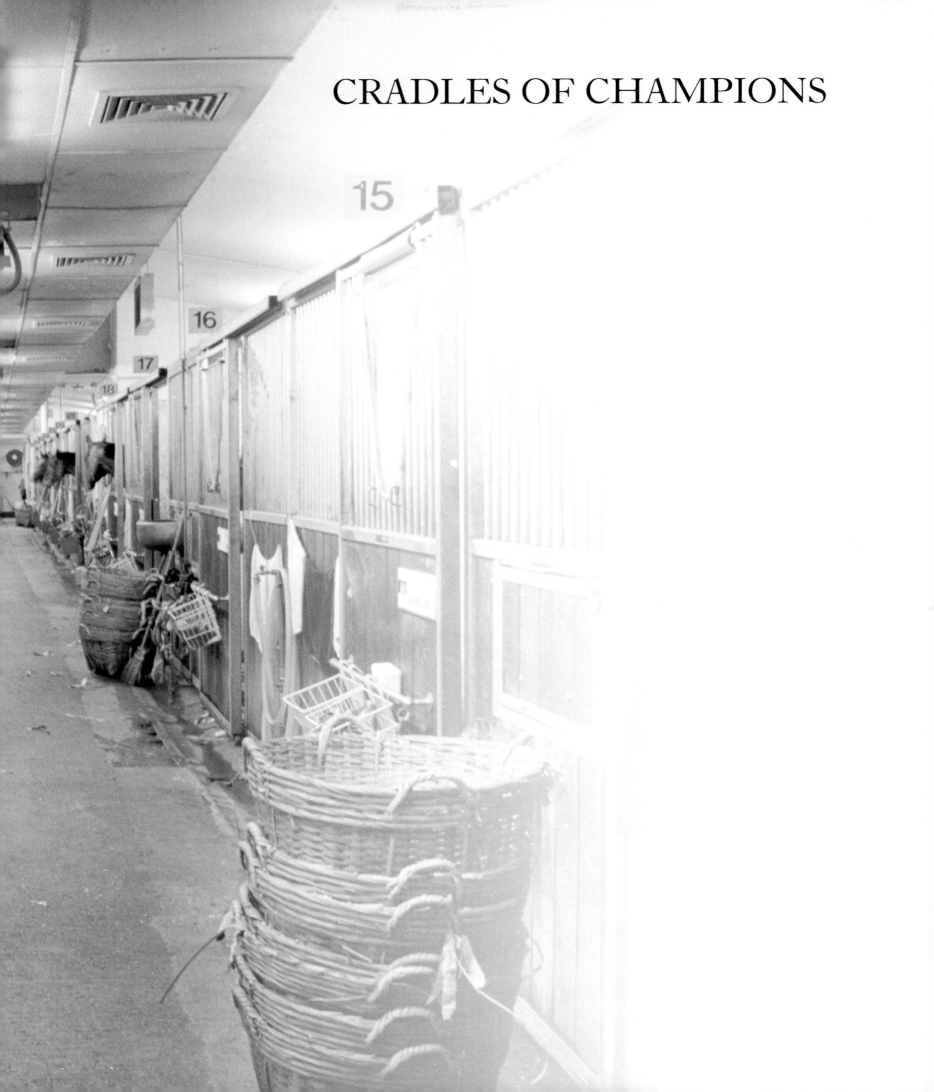

CRADLES OF CHAMPIONS

THE CALUMET SAGA Lexington, Kentucky

IN SEARCH OF THE AMERICAN CRADLE of racehorses, we follow our guiding star deep into the heart of Kentucky, tracking signposts that lead to the great horse farms of English thoroughbreds. Finally in the distance we catch sight of the famous slate roofs, but we still have farther to go along the miles of white fencing that surround the stud farm. Once we go through the entrance gate to Calumet Farm, we stand in the heart of an American myth. We enter not only a temple of breeding but also a universe in which the very walls are legendary. From glory to downfall, the Calumet Farm epic is one of the great American success stories.

Calumet Farm is the archetype of American agricultural architecture in every way, from its vast fields to the smallest details of its construction. The stand-alone barns, made of wood or brick and found throughout agricultural regions of the eastern United States, are one of the key aspects of its architectural heritage. In addition, from a distance, the perspectives of the great slate roofs, topped with dovecotes, bathe the inside of the stables with light. The barns are the symbol of Calumet and provide a model for the architecture of many stables around the world. This faithfulness to a regional rural architecture, developed with great luxury and refinement, is Calumet Farm's signature style.

The story of one of the most beautiful stables in the United States began in 1924—with a baking powder factory! That year, William Monroe Wright established the Calumet Baking Powder Company, a rapid commercial success that soon allowed him to dedicate himself entirely to what he modestly called his "little trotter farm." The small farm did well and expanded to include gallopers, which initially brought the owners great wealth before eventually leading to bankruptcy. Constantly thrown from one excess to the other, the story of Calumet Farm is marked by family dramas and base desires.

Opposite, below, and page 82: Behind the white fences, the mythical home of racehorse breeding stretches over more than 300 hectares. The fact that Calumet Farm's reputation extends beyond the boundaries of Kentucky comes as much from its thoroughbreds results at the finishing post as from the beauty of its buildings. The price of this success, however, has been the rumors surrounding the farm and its turbulent history.

What should Calumet Farm be remembered for—its dramatic history, built on passion and money, a model of the twists and turns of an American saga? Or for the stud farm buildings, which represent an architectural ideal in so many ways? Calumet Farm is an extraordinary stable on both accounts, an expression of the secret alchemy, the subtle equilibrium and the implacability of the American myth of rise and fall.

For several decades after 1930, the green fields of Calumet Farm enjoyed a season of good fortune, and the Wright family passion was crowned with success. Their horses were increasingly dominant at the finishing post. The estate grew, and with it came ever more red and white barns.

In the 1980s, however, the apparent flourishing of this idyllic setting was no longer enough to quash the rumors. Was it simply jealousy, or was it fair criticism? In any event, harsh critics accused the Wright family of having transformed the most beautiful animals in the world into mere cash dispensers. A scandal broke out concerning Alydar, the greatest champion horse of his generation. Taken out of competition, in 1990 he had to be put down due to an injury. Some commentators began to speculate about the insurance policy taken out on the champion horse. The insurance company brought a lawsuit against Calumet Farm and won the case against the inheritor of the Wright dynasty for insurance fraud and bribery.

Without family leadership, Calumet Farm fell into crisis. Crippled with debts, the farm was in dire straights. Would the American empire of English thoroughbreds recover from this scandal? Who would now take care of Calumet's proud legacy?

Miracles exist, and Calumet proves it. The savior, Henryk de Kwiatkowski, came from many miles away, and his journey was long and fantastic. Was it a fabrication or was it the truth? On the surface, his biography was entirely improbable, even if it was the very stuff of the "American dream."

Calumet Farm is the American dream: the farm was created in the 1920s by a small businessman who made a fortune in the American food-processing industry; in just a few years his dazzling rise allowed him to take his passion for gallopers to such a level of excellence that Calumet thoroughbreds ruled the racetracks right up to the 1980s.

Born in Poland, Henryk de Kwiatkowski was imprisoned in Siberia at age fifteen, after the Russian invasion. Two years later, he escaped the camp and made his way to Iran. From there, he set off for Great Britain by sea. His boat was hit by a torpedo, and he was the sole survivor among the four hundred passengers. Once in London, he joined the Royal Air Force and was involved in many missions. After the war, he became a broker for aircraft fleets for the most powerful men on the planet, supplying, among others, the Shah of Iran with combat planes. Apparently, in 1953, he even saved the Shah from an attempted coup d'état.

These incredible adventures made Henryk de Kwiatowski something of a James Bond. The big-hearted hero amassed a considerable fortune, which he used to buy Calumet Farm in 1992, saving it from bankruptcy. He revived the horse farm, adding a polo field, which can be admired from the air when landing at the nearby airport in Lexington.

Henryk de Kwiatkowski died in 2003. But the Calumet saga is not yet over: his family is determined to keep the story going. The jockey uniform at Calumet Farm – red jersey, blue armband, and red cap – is still a point of reference on the American racetrack; the Calumet colts are still frolicking on the hills of the estate; and white fences still run through the rolling green fields of Kentucky.

Right and above: White walls, sliding doors with red uprights, and dovecotes that pour soft light down into the stables . . . the Calumet buildings' silhouette is very familiar, a source of inspiration for many European stud farms, that have imitated its simple, elegant lines.

Following pages: Inside the barns, the stalls are arranged on either side of a wide central aisle. Today, this arrangement is the one favored by the greatest breeders in the world, in preference to traditional stables where the stalls look outward, without any neighbors opposite. Here, the horses are face to face, reassured by the presence of one another. This ensures the precious alchemy that makes these exceptional mounts racing champions by avoiding unnecessary distress.

Above: Presentation leads and saddle carpets in Calumet Farm's colors.

Right: Warm Kentucky light illuminates the interior of the stables, warming the heart of the horses, and of those who take care of them. Here, everything reflects peace and excellence—two words that define the atmosphere of Calumet Farm and make the place so fascinating.

BEFORE THE RACE,
KILDANGAN STUD FARM

County Kildare, Ireland

IN THE SLANTING LIGHT OF AUTUMN, across frosty fields, lone walkers slip between the trees as they wind their way up and down the paths of a stud farm. They dream of young colts, their fragile promise for a victorious future, snorting noisily and moving off, away from the white fences surrounding the racetrack. Yellow and ocher leaves in the trees are a counterpoint to the coats of the thoroughbreds; red leaves burn against the horses' copper tinged chestnut coats. All around, there is a natural tranquility. The frail and frisky legs of the foals stand juxtaposed against the quiet strength of the oak trees in the park. The connections are omnipresent, clear as day, as Kildangan deploys its easy, almost shameless, beauty.

In 1986, when Sheikh Al Maktoum decided to establish his Irish breeding ground at Kildangan, was he conscious of giving the young colts, these mere yearlings, such a deep historical heritage, such age-old serenity? He must have listened to the song of the trees, the intimacy of the kind and gentle nature, in the colors of wood and the rounded meadows; he must have heard the spirit of Kildangan.

Kildangan is inhabited by spirits, the spirit of the forest and the spirit of a creature escaped from the rich bestiary of Celtic myth. Kildangan Stud Farm is filled with spirits in every corner, inspiring every foal born here.

The magnificent entrance driveway, lined with hundred-year-old trees, is only a foretaste of an estate that has been dedicated to horse breeding since the 1930s. Mother Nature settles comfortably all around the castle and cemetery, pushing aside gray granite Celtic crosses. When the horses first arrived, the great oaks, beeches, horse chestnuts, and hornbeams bore witness to a new generation of occupants. But these are not ordinary horses: they are

Previous page and below: County Kildare has been favored by horse breeders for many years; in 1986, Sheik Al Maktoum decided to settle his colts there. He bought a hundred-year-old stud farm, adding modern buildings that remain faithful to the original style.

Left: The gates of the main stables open onto the office. An entire breeding microcosm thrives in this verdant setting. The stallions that serve at Kildangan are some of the most expensive in the world, costing some $50,000 each.

Systematic and efficient; just like the breeding, the training of the colts has a sole objective: to produce tomorrow's champions. Soon they will leave their green pastures for the racetrack.

champions, gallopers, destined to fire up the greatest race-tracks in the world. In the great Kildangan park, the colts soon became an integral part of a harmonious whole, as if the serenity of the place soothed the horses' frailty.

When Sheikh Al Maktoum bought Kildangan Estate in 1986, Irish breeders were worried about the direction the farm would take under the leadership of this unusual enthusiast from Dubai. They were concerned that a farm that had remained traditional for so long would be industrialized. Sheik Al Maktoum already owned stud farms in the United States, Australia, and Great Britain. What would he understand about the subtle methods known only in the deep valleys of County Kildare, born of the experience of many generations? They were afraid he would impose a pace and methods in conflict with the Irish and their landscape.

Today, the spirit of Kildangan is at peace again. Sheikh Al Maktoum chose to design the stables in the American style, with barns spread all over the estate. They stand along the edges of the fields, a dozen large, long, white buildings, with slate roofs topped with a dovecote that sheds gentle light down through a central corridor. Showing great respect for the local area, the modern stables are arranged around older buildings, using materials and forming silhouettes familiar to County Kildare. They offer a calm and sensitive homage to the spirit of Kildangan.

Yet a strange absence hangs over the farm, for the horses are hidden, as if sheltered from the cold. From the thick-leaved oak to the purple beech, from the meadow to the pen, from the racetrack to the entrance gate, one unanswered question remains: where are the horses?

Far from the crowd, wide driveways lead up to brick buildings. The dominant shapes of rare botanical species brought back from the edge of the world in the nineteenth century still stand out in the park. As the seasons pass, their foliage changes color dramatically.

The walker scans the fields, but finds no answer. In the near distance, herds of cows and sheep, those inglorious, docile ruminants, work hard at keeping short the six hundred hectares of the estate, with a regularity that defies the most modern mowers! Thanks to the sheep, the grass is kept at an ideal length for the horses.

The intrigued wanderers retraces their footsteps, towards the stud farm's ancient core. They see the Celtic crosses bent over with the years, after five centuries of protecting the first occupants of the estate from invisible predators with their granite strength. Finally, just behind the cemetery, they catch sight of the old stone stables. During their daily exercise, the stallions walk to Kildangan Castle, a grand, gray estate, full of majestic melancholy.

Once again the walker becomes lost in the park's woody groves; they wander under a flaming horse chestnut tree, looks up its great trunk, and is deeply moved by such secular benevolence. This natural kingdom is a paradise for the horses, bringing everything together to ensure that each colt is given the best chance.

Eventually they come across the colts in the stud farm's eight modern stables. The shape of the buildings is inspired by the agricultural structures of classic American architecture. At Kildangan, as on the other side of the Atlantic, slate roofs and sober lines and colors are reminiscent of the simplicity of the first nineteenth-century American family farms. But Ireland is also present in these stables, for the walls are made of brick, like the local architecture on Kildangan Estate. Across the rooftops of the stables, weathervanes punctuate the skyline and lines of perspective meet; the vaulted arches join harmoniously, framed by gray granite porches that anchor the stables in the region. The spirit of Kildangan shines through, more potent than ever.

Spread all over the 600-hectare estate, the stables have various different layouts. In one, the buildings open onto a horseshoe shaped courtyard (above); elsewhere they are spread around a square courtyard. In the barns seen in the distance, the stalls face each other.

Right and following pages: An encounter between precious creatures and a legendary land. This fertile combination offers the ideal conditions for horses to thrive, some of which will leave their mark in history.

WITH ANNUAL SALES OF ALMOST $20 BILLION, the Hong Kong Jockey Club has shown record profits. This lucrative operation allows its directors to maintain two of the most sophisticated racetracks and most elaborate stable in the world. To find horses lodged like princes is a paradox that flies in the face of this densely populated city where every single square foot is accounted for. Yet far from the noise, bustle, and bright lights of the city, 1,200 horses live right in the heart of the built up area, housed in buildings that stretch all along a canal. Every one of the 1,200 champion horses requires intensive training and specialized care. Faced with extreme spatial pressures, the Hong Kong Jockey Club came up with a unique solution: alongside the racetrack grandstand was built an ultra-modern stable three stories high, a marvel of technology and spatial economy.

Once a horse comes through the entrance tunnel to the building, it begins its contribution to an experience that is oriented toward a single goal: earning huge sums of money by winning races.

One thousand two hundred horses living on three stories! Like everyone else in Hong Kong, even the inhabitants of stables must conform to the demands of the city. Nature is completely mastered in this vertical realm. To give just one example, the bedding in the stalls is made of paper, a forage that has many advantages. To start with the question of supplies: manufactured goods are far more readily available in Hong Kong than natural products. Paper is cut into strips that are exactly a foot long, a specific length that avoids getting wrapped around the horses' legs. The paper is printed like newspapers because the ink deters the horses from eating the strips, thus ensuring total

Previous page: An island of green surrounded by skyscrapers; the presence of the Sha Tin racetrack right in the heart of Hong Kong is a paradox. On one side, a gambling temple; on the other, a high-tech complex: the Hong Kong Jockey Club is a world of its own.

Opposite: Space is a rare commodity in one of the most densely populated cities in the world. Just like the housing complexes, the stables are on several floors. To reach their stalls, horses walk up and down ramps.

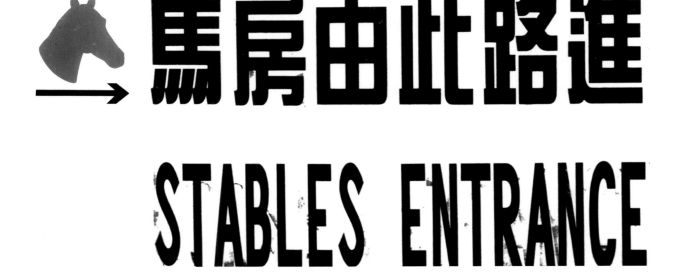

馬房由此路進
STABLES ENTRANCE

control over their feeding. Furthermore, in these air-conditioned stables, paper bedding does not make any dust. When the champions get bored in their golden prison, plastic toys are hung in their stalls to distract them.

Just like good citizens, the horses move from one floor to another in the elevator, which they reach via a system of ramps and narrow corridors. There are swimming pools worthy of the smartest gyms, a solarium, specialist clinics, and treadmills. In short, the residents of the Hong Kong Jockey Club enjoy every attention and care, and they never need to leave the club's arena. Only at the end of their careers, when they leave the Club to spend their retirement outside the city, do they gain the right to admire the sky and the green grass of the fields.

The stables have been entirely transformed since the Hong Kong Jockey Club was founded in 1884. The site was a challenge from the start, as the marshes were the only flat area in the whole of the island. After draining this area, the city's first racetrack was built on it. One race a year used to take place on the Chinese New Year, started by the English colonists. Soon it became a defining event of the sporting and social calendar of the colony. The Chinese, who have always loved animal competition, quickly caught onto betting fever with the horses. Other races were organized by private companies and managed by the Hong Kong Jockey Club. However, this was not the primary vocation of one of the most select clubs in Hong Kong: only very powerful institutions can take on the breeding

The Hong Kong Jockey Club makes the most of every precious square foot: in the center of the racetrack are large circular walkers where the horses warm up before training sessions.

Sunday afternoon in the Hong Kong Jockey Club arena: the haven of green turns into an effervescent arena. Day and night, the Hong Kong races attract all kinds of punters who all come to lose themselves in gaming fever.

and training of racehorses, since independent private stables can never be assured of sufficient financial stability. The Club has remained loyal to its initial purpose since the late nineteenth century.

Places in the stables are rare and expensive: to secure a stall, owners must become members of the Club through sponsorship and election. Above all, they must supply solid bank references to prove that they can pay the annual boarding fee of almost $100,000 for their champion horse.

With nearly seven hundred races a year, the track never rests: in the morning, the horses in the Club take turns training; in the afternoon the track is handed over to the races. The most spectacular races take place all week long at night, when the inside of the racetrack becomes an arena of light and speed where every year more than a million people come to lay their bets. Surprising as it might seem, the Club remains a nonprofit organization, redistributing all its profits to charitable organizations. In this temple of triumphant capitalism, the technological excellence of the stables is thus paired with a unique philanthropic agenda.

The Hong Kong Jockey Club ensures great training facilities for its champions: a gently graded swimming pool and powerful showers to massage the athletes' muscles. The care here is as attentive as in an exclusive spa.

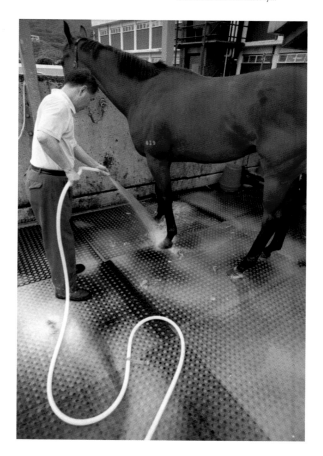

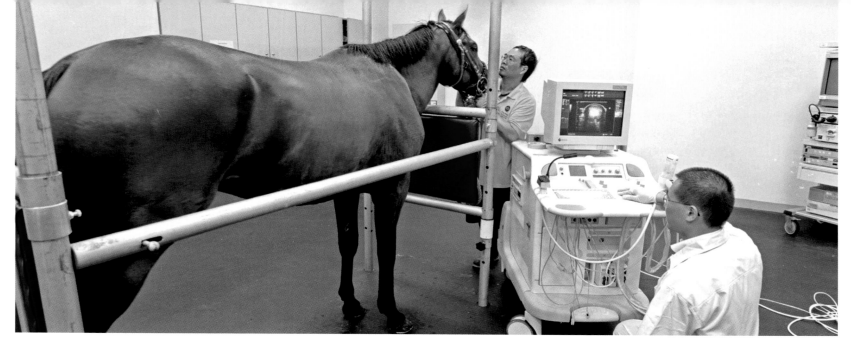

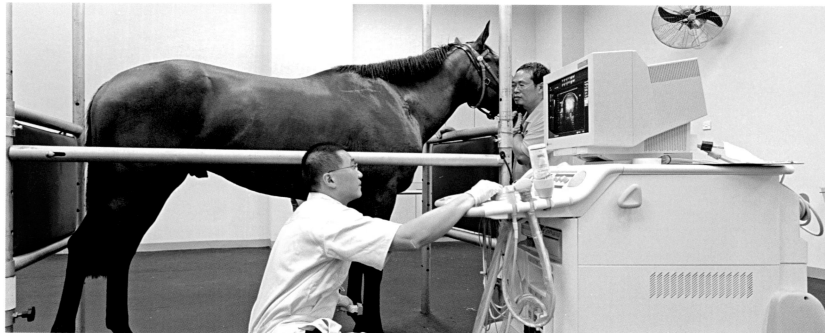

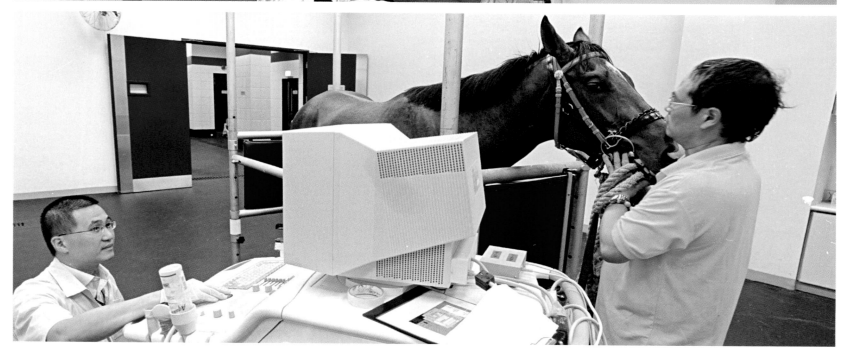

子彈火車
BULLET TRAIN

Above: Thunder Bolt's stall, like those of each of the 1,200 horses in the Hong Kong Jockey Club, is filled with thin strips of paper: this technique allows careful surveillance of the champion horses' feeding and avoids dust in the stables.

Left: Two trainers use a computer to perform an ultrasound: Thunder Bolt's tendons, worth their weight in gold, must be cared for appropriately.

Next pages: On the third floor of their ivory tower, King of Fish, Liverbird, and Good to Great take a break from their full schedule: a few hours of rest before they enter the starting box.

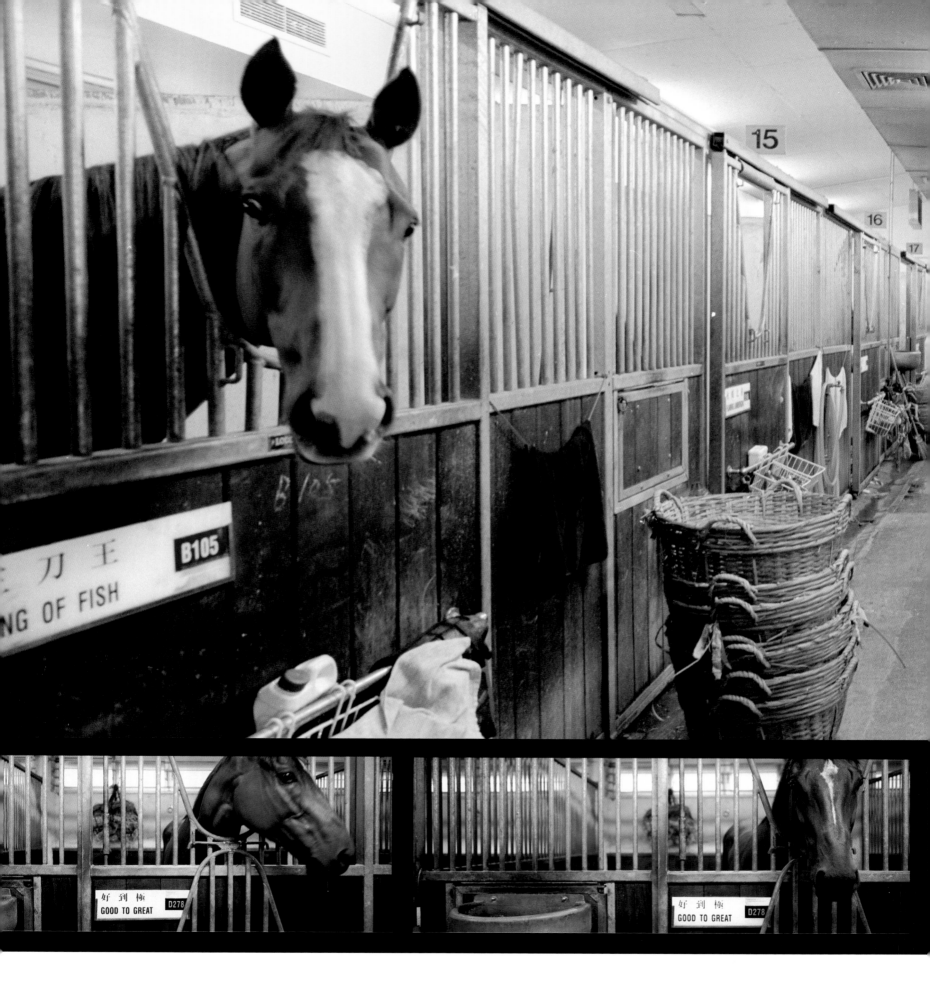

MARBACH NATIONAL STATE STUD FARM

Baden-Würtemberg, Germany

ONCE VISITORS ENTER THE HEAVY IRON GATEWAY bearing a finely gilded insignia, they stand on the premises of Marbach National State Stud Farm in the Baden-Württemberg region of Germany. The emblematic seal, hailed as a proof of excellence throughout Germany, is branded on the thigh of every horse born here.

The estate, owned by the commune of Gomadingen, stretches over thousands of hectares and is divided into four separate entities. The stud itself consists of seventeen main buildings in addition to the stables, including the farrier outhouses, stud museum, riding halls, hayloft, and coach houses where astounding collector's pieces stand next to more contemporary carriages.

To the left of the main entrance, opening onto a vast central courtyard, is the English Stable, an impressive stable for stallions. The gray stone building, topped with a bell tower, was built in 1840 for Duke Christophe of Württemburg's racehorses. A thick-walled building on the right is the oldest part of the stud farm. It was originally constructed around 1600 and now serves as the main office and private residence of the stud farm director.

Each of the buildings surrounding the main courtyard reflects an individual architectural style. Strong, solid stone buildings stand next to typical local style wooden buildings. The focal point of all these architectural juxtapositions is the half-timbered facade on the second floor of the main stables. In the center of the courtyard, the famous stud fountain stands proud, surmounted by a delicate sculpture of a mare suckling her foal. Built in 1844 to water the horses on the estate, today the fountain alone represents all the grandeur of Marbach.

Previous page: A romantic vision of the traditional riding ring, covered with vines, built between 1854 and 1860. Inside, under the wooden ceiling, there is a wonderfully calm atmosphere.

The stalls for the stallions under great roofs covered with snow. In the old Offenhausen monastery, there is an artificial insemination clinic.

Previous pages: The "Vorwerk Güterstei"
is a typical example of Black Forest
architecture, with solid wooden beams
and carved stone. This ancient Cistercian
monastery dating back to the twelfth
century is used today for the young fillies.

Left: Arab stallion stall decorated with
old lamps.

The South stable at Marbach is famous throughout the world for its superb Arab horses. They are the last lineages known in Europe, dating back to the period of King Frederic II. Its stud-book begins in 1817.

As the gates of the large stable for the magnificent Arab mares open, they offer a spectacular moment as the horses step out onto snowy ground.

The fountain with a sculpture showing a mare suckling her colt is one of the symbols of the stud farm. All the horses in the stable are watered here before returning to their stalls.

Right: The Dominican monastery, dating back to the early thirteenth century, is built in the Gothic style. It is the center of the Offenhausen stud farm.

Below: The old bell tower of the English Stable has a special bell, with a distinctive low ring, to signal when it is time to stop work for meals.

Aside from the stables, the farm buildings include a charming small, wooden-roofed manège and a vast modern riding ring that seats thousands of spectators. The stud welcomes more than 300,000 visitors a year. The architecture of all these buildings blends functionality with tradition, as in the amazing wooden five-story building that acts as a "fodder loft" and in the open stables that house the mares and their foals at night. Unlike royal stables, the stallions' stables are not open for visitors, and in the muffled enclosure of the boxes, the horses share an intimacy that encourages their reproduction.

The farm annexes at Marbach are about seven miles from the main stud. Nowadays all the foals are raised at Güterstein, on the land of a former Cistercian monastery built in the twelfth century, while the young mares are kept on the grounds of an old forester and hunter lodge dedicated to St. John. The stud also acquired the former Dominican monastery at Offenhausen, built in early gothic style, next to a church dating back to the beginning of the thirteenth century. This is the site of the insemination center, as well as a stable for the famous Schwartzwälder, the Black Forest draft horses. This unique breed found only in Baden-Württemberg, the descendant of rustic Noriker horses, nowadays has a long, pale mane that is the result of many years of breeding with local mares.

For many centuries, Marbach stud farm represented the summit of German equitation, and it has lost none of its brilliance today. Yet over time the estate has faced many vicissitudes. Destroyed and ransacked on many different occasions, only the administrative buildings were able to resist the attacks of looters and violent conflicts. Founded in the early sixteenth century and today the oldest of the ten national German studs that are still active,

Herd of racehorses grazing in front of an old six-floor grain storage barn, built entirely of wood. This is where fodder is stored during the winter.

Marbach is a witness of history. A chronicle from 1568 refers to the "stables built on the lands of Marbach by Duke Christophe of Württemberg to house his most valiant race horses . . . . These stables were admired by many crowned visitors who came to the estate . . . ." The stud was first destroyed in 1634, during the Thirty Year War. In 1812, King Frederick II of Prussia established nearly 90,000 horses and an elite cavalry regiment t at Marbach. The crushing defeat of the Prussian armies in Russia during the Napoleonic wars left Marbach drained. Nevertheless, the stud reemerged once again. In 1817, another highly skilled horseman, the King of Baden-Württemberg, made a priceless gift to the stud when he introduced several horses imported from the Arabian Peninsula, including Bairactar. Marbach consequently became the first stud in Europe involved in the breeding of Arab thoroughbreds, the venerable fathers of the most illustrious European lineages.

Most of the horses on the stud are stallions, and are primarily racehorses born at Marbach, the worthy descendants of the most prestigious European pedigrees. Training and trotting sessions take place in the forest or in the more modern riding ring buildings. Young, highly spirited from all over the region come to Marbach to take part in stallions tests. Every year the stud, which is undoubtedly one of the best trainer and horse-breaker schools, organizes a racehorse auction, during which time it also presents many equestrian events, from dressage competitions to obstacle races.

Apart from all facts and anecdotes, Marbach is legendary throughout Germany. Its rigor and professionalism are linked to a passion for horses that has evolved in perfect harmony with nature on historic, ancient lands, bearers of deep emotion.

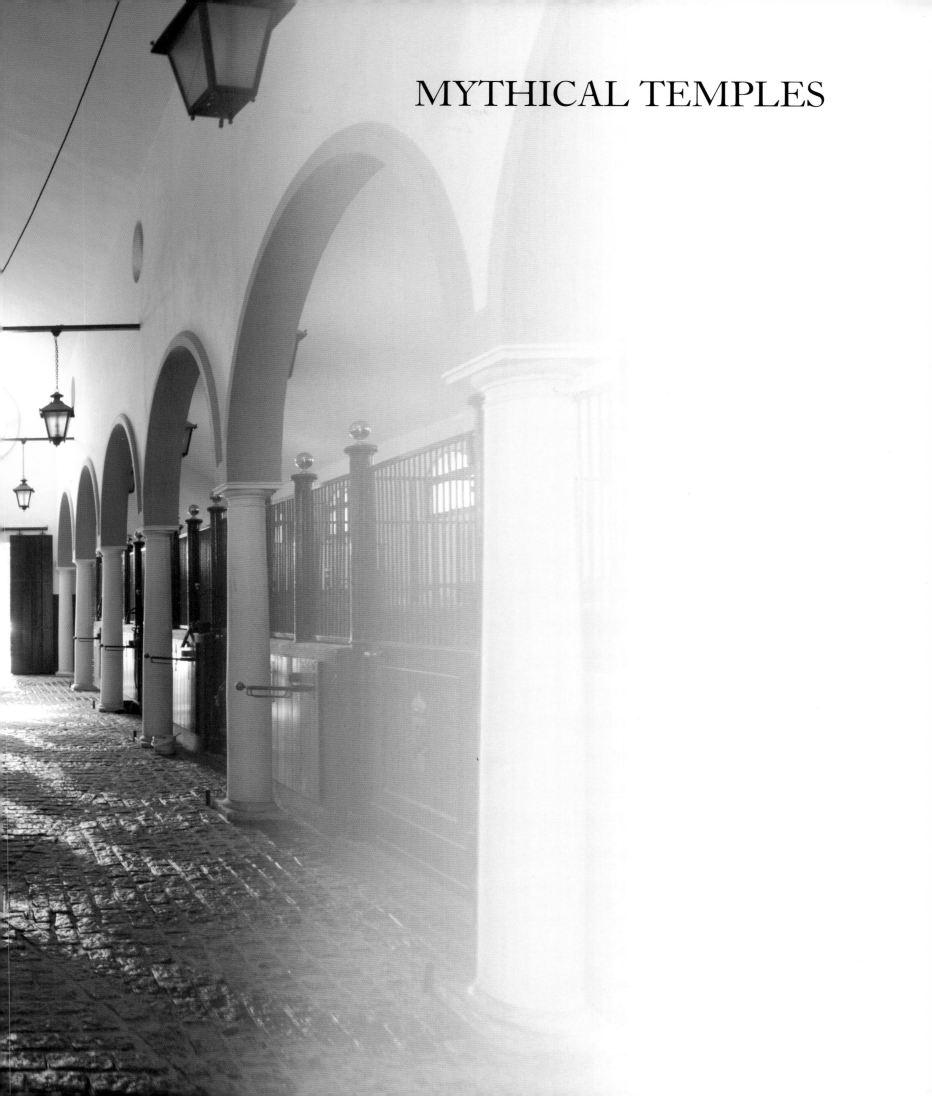

MYTHICAL TEMPLES

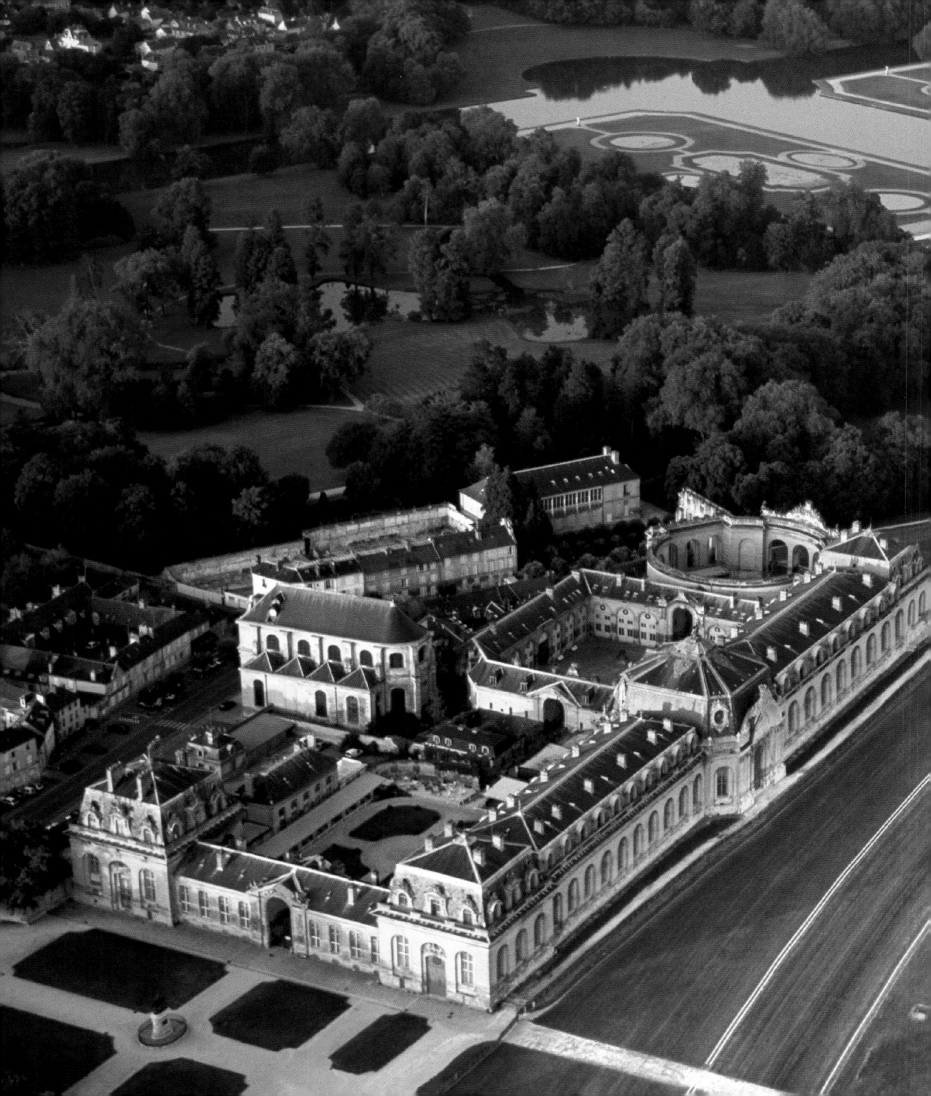

THE STABLE PALACE Chantilly, France

OUGHT WE TO BELIEVE THE LEGENDARY CLAIM that Louis-Henri de Bourbon, Seventh Prince de Condé, convinced that he would be reincarnated as a horse, sought to build the most beautiful stables in the world? The Chantilly Stables are stunning in their majesty, constituting an entirely separate, unique palace.

Where else in the world does one find stables so far from the master's residence? The stables at Versailles are integral to the arrangement of the whole, forming the curve of the Place d'armes, in the wings that follow the main avenues leading up to the palace. But Chantilly is quite different: by placing the stables on the edge of a vast lawn, which is nowadays the racetrack, architect Jean Aubert bravely disconnected completely the stable building from the existing castle, which stands proudly surrounded by water. Aubert created an entirely independent building that stands alone, on its own terms.

In 1619, when the presentation of the initial designs received immediate success and approval, Aubert was welcomed into the Royal Architectural Academy. The foundation stone was laid on May 16, 1721, and by 1736 the monumental building was fully built, provoking much surprise and enduring admiration for its innovation, luxury, generous size, and appearance.

The vast building that houses the stables stretches over more than two hundred yards, along the racetrack. In the eighteenth century, it housed the stalls reserved for Prince de Condé's hunting horses, as well as his carriage horses. It has two long naves, which come together in a large octagon and end in two pavilions that are slightly set back. Each nave holds 120 horses, arranged along one wide, central aisle. The courtyards and outbuildings necessary for the upkeep of a large hunt stand behind these. A passageway links the western nave to the first kennel,

Previous page: "These stables are ridiculously beautiful; the building is more elaborate than the palaces of several kings together." This acerbic remark, no doubt an expression of extreme jealousy, is perhaps the best description of the gesture behind Chantilly Stables: they form an entirely separate monument, standing in splendid isolation, as if turning their back on the castle off in the neighboring reflecting pool.

Opposite: Louis Henri de Bourbon, Seventh Prince de Condé, placed great value on hunting. The sculptures decorating the stables are reminders of his passion: horses, stags, wild boars, hounds, and hunting trophies are all represented on the pediments and inside the stables. In addition to the stalls, boxes, and other horse-related rooms, the building included five kennels..

141

Previous pages: The squat silhouette of the Chantilly Stables: slate roofs; rounded tympanums; bas-reliefs of wild horses, some fiery, others resting peacefully in a natural landscape; supporting walls along the facade; and even the winged victory statue perched high on the central pavilion—together these elements evoke the classical harmony sought by architect Aubert, who was highly respected by his peers and an admiring public.

Right: Life has changed dramatically at Chantilly. After the Revolution, the stables were requisitioned by the army, and these days hunting parties no longer gather there. One day when he noticed a horse galloping across the esplanade in front of the stables, the Duke d'Aumale had the idea of setting up a racetrack. Today, the Chantilly hippodrome comes ablaze during one of the most important galloping races, and the town is still one of the main centers for racehorses.

which opens onto a courtyard. There were five kennels altogether: one for the stag hounds, one for the females, one for wild boar hounds, a winter kennel, and a kennel for sick dogs. A double arcade separates this courtyard from the sheds and the forge.

The Condés adored hunting. Their dual passion for hunting and horses is omnipresent in the rich decorations of the constructions they devoted to them: architectural ornaments, bas-reliefs, frescoes, and elaborate scenes sculpted around inner fountains. On the pediments of the entrance portal, horses rear up over packs of hounds; the dormer windows are replete with hunting and battle trophies. On the rooftop of the central pavilion a Renommée on horseback takes to the sky in a lead copy of Coyzevox's marble sculpture for Marly's drinking trough. Behind the double nave of the stables, other annexes housed the carriages and poste-chaise, as well as the tack and harness rooms. Beside the road leading to the castle is an open riding arena, surrounded by the elegant curves of sumptuous arcades. Nothing was too grand or too fine for the Prince de Condé's horses. In 1754, this openly flaunted magnificence caused the Prince de Ligne to comment, no doubt with a hint of jealousy: "these stables are ridiculously beautiful; the building is more elaborate than the palaces of several kings together."

The grandeur of the stables derives not only from their unusual size, but also from their perfect proportions. Even though their vault is more than forty feet above the ground, the stables give the impression of a fairly squat building and their design remains quite classical. The mantels of the twenty-nine windows that line the facade emphasize the horizontal plane between the pavilions at either end. The octagon sits in the center, rounded on the inside to form a dome that is lit by large oculi, decorated with the heads of stags and wild boars. On the outside, the building's prominent position shows it off in all its splendor. Its tympanum, on which wild horses stand out in a bas-relief, is dominated by a high archivolt, with alternating vessels and lions. Under the rooftops, behind the rows of

Beneath the roofs of the main gallery and the annexes, three generations of stable hands were kept busy caring for the Princes de Condé's horses. Today, thanks to the Musée Vivant du Cheval, the Living Museum of Horses, the stables are still full of equestrian activity, and the lofty vaults of the main gallery become crowded before every spectacle as the horses make their way toward the riding ring.

dormer windows, apart from the hay and straw lofts, there are also the apartments for the stable hands and all the other personnel dedicated to the upkeep of the horses: the stable master, forager, gunsmith, farrier, stable boys, grooms, coachmen, and postillions. In all, three generations lived there.

The great lawn and the surrounding forests rang with the sounds of hunting horns and hunting parties chasing after stags and wild boars. Festivities kept the magnificent buildings alight, and they became the culmination for evening promenades. The court came to Chantilly Stables from Versailles. Emperor Joseph II of Habsborg, Marie Antoinette's father, and the Grand Duke Paul, future Tsar Paul I, as well as Prussian Prince Henry, were all seen there.

The year 1789 rang the death knell for the extravagant hunting parties and the memorable festivities held at Chantilly. The lead ornaments were soon pillaged and taken to Paris to be melted down. Police regiments, and later dragoons, moved into the magnificent buildings, adapting them to their needs. During the Restoration and Empire, the great huntsman from the Condé family visited only occasionally. The great lawn saw its first galloping races, and the fixed grandstands, built in 1881, were inaugurated by the Duke d'Aumale. After he was sent into political exile, the duke bequeathed his stables and the entire estate to the state in 1897.

Today, the stables house the Living Museum of Horses. In reflection of its past splendor, Chantilly is still a center for horses. The great lawn still trembles with the excitement of some of the most famous galloping races, such as the Diane Prize and the Jockey-Club Prize, and to this day the golden vault of the Prince de Condé's stables resonates with the whinnying of impatient horses.

At Chantilly, stone still stands and history remains intact. Behind the double nave of the stables, an open riding ring is surrounded by sumptuous arcades, where many horse shows take place even today.

THE STABLES OF UDAIPUR Kingdom of Mewar, India

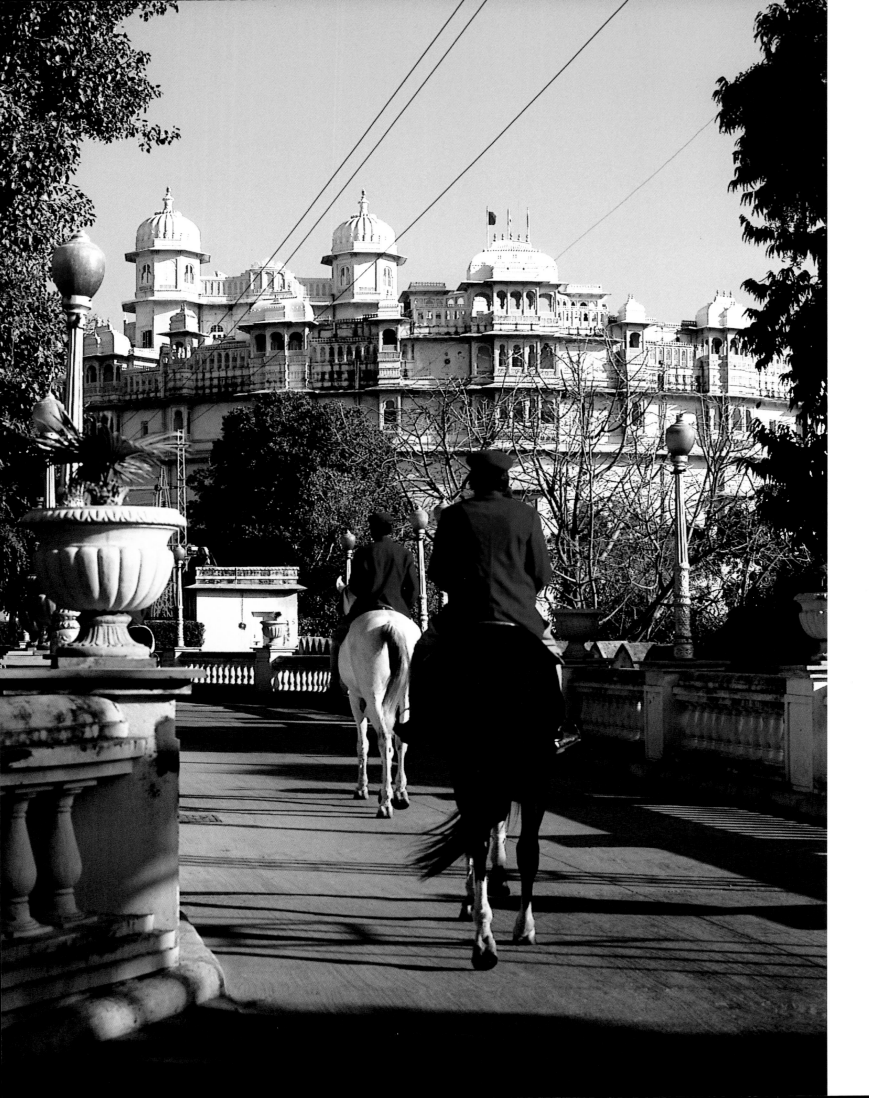

LAND OF LEGEND, MYTH AND MYSTICISM, India never ceases to amaze and enchant us. The history of the Udaipur Palace stables is steeped in tradition and deep emotions that transport us beyond rational thought. This history is a hidden sap or secret essence. Tourist guides never mention the Udaipur Palace stables, nestled deep in the heart of the sumptuous residence of the region's greatest dynasty, yet the stables' symbolic importance make this a truly fascinating and extraordinary site.

Udaipur Palace, which overlooks the town below, is a fortress of pale stone. At sunset, its silhouette drowns in a great lake, seeped in the last golden rays of the sun. Behind these high walls hide the stables of the royal house of Mewar, in southern Rajasthan, land of epic splendor.

According to myth, the Maharanas of Mewar are descendants of the Sun God, via the son of Ram; their history is told in the Ramayana. This sacred line endows the Mewar dynasty with the much admired title of Maharana. The House of Mewar ruled for more than 1,400 years.

The city of Udaipur was founded in 1559 when Rana Udaï Singh II came on a horse, hunting on the bank of Lake Pichola. Udaï Singh II met a saddhu who advised him to build his palace right on this bank. At that time, the north of India was torn apart by internal wars: bloody battles followed local skirmishes. Without their horses, the Rajputs would never have survived. Miniatures on display in the palace remind us of the omnipresence of horses in that era. Whether on the battlefield, the hunting ground, or expeditions, or as leaders of men, the Maharanas of Udaipur are invariably represented on their mounts. Even their puppet equivalents (Udaipur is one of the great centers

Previous page: In Southern Rajasthan stands Udaipur Palace, the royal residency of the House of Mewar, the oldest Rajput dynasty.

Left: The stables are found in the very heart of the palace. Every day, the horses follow a precise itinerary; their morning walk brings them before the Maharana for a detailed inspection in an immutable, daily ritual.

Right: Below the palace, on the edge of Lake Pichola, an enclosure enables the Maharana's five Marwari horses to exercise. Occasionally Princess Bhargavi Mewar, the Maharana's daughter, who is a great horse enthusiast, rides them.

of the art of puppetry) depict the Maharanas astride their stallions.

This history helps us understand why the center of the palace, the very heart of the building, has always been reserved for the stables. The stables are preserved in this arabesque jewel of marble, surrounded by the Mardana Mahal (the men's palace), the Zenana Mahal (the women's apartment), and the Surya Gokhra ("the sun loggia"). The stables form the point of convergence from any given perspective, allowing the entire court, from the masters of the palace down, to contemplate their mounts in the sweep of an eye.

Yet what is most striking about the stables is their simplicity. All around them, in the pavilions and shady courtyards, brightly hued enamels, stained glass, and gold draw the eye to the smallest detail, while the stables display none of this decorative profusion. Compared to the sumptuous buildings of the palace, the stables are also remarkably small, now housing just five horses. They are airy, allowing precious breezes to circulate during heat waves and the monsoon. A permanently cool stone roof protects the horses from the sun, and one entire stable wall opens generously onto a shady courtyard. The building is striking on account of the sobriety of its decor: virgin white walls present a surprising austerity in a country in which pictorial art is ubiquitous. Only the massive grey pillars, whose capitals are sculpted with floral motifs, depart from the sparse style of this haven of tranquility. When the sun caresses the columns with its amber rays, the granite sparkles from the depths of the stables.

Elsewhere in the region, this type of column is normally found in sacred temples. This is what makes the

Previous pages and opposite: Once many hundreds defended the borders of the kingdom; now there are just five stables in the city palace. Ever since they were built, some several hundred years ago, these stables have housed the Maharana's five most magnificent horses: they embody power, courage, and nobility. Today Raj Tilak, Ganesh, Chance, Raj Roop, and Raj Ratan are the horses that live in the palace's stables. They are the pride of their master, Maharana Arvind Singh Mewar, of Udaipur.

Udaipur Palace stables so extraordinary, evoking a deep, quasi-mystical symbolism.

Raj Tilak, Ganesh, Chance, Raj Roop, and Raj Ratan, the five protégés of Shree Arvind Singh, the current Maharana, play an important role in the life of the palace. They embody the attributes of power. As demi-gods linked to the House of Mewar's authority, these figures contribute to the social equilibrium. The horses participate in religious ceremonies and palace rituals partly because of a deep-seated admiration of their appearance, but also because they support and protect those in power. Indeed, the ceremony of Ashwan Pooja (*Pooja* means "blessing" or "prayer") is dedicated entirely to the horses.

Ashwan Pooja takes place in October. For an entire morning, hidden in the stables, grooms dress the horses with beautiful cloths and decorate them with a thousand and one jewels. A precise vocabulary has evolved to designate each of these jewels: *halra*, the silver collar decorated with flowers and a peacock in silver filigree; *kilingi*, the golden feather tuft placed between the curved ears of Marwari horses; *neveri*, a silver bracelet worn above the knee; and *dumchi*, a decoration crafted from leather encrusted with silver, secured by the saddle and placed beneath the tail.

Bedecked in their most beautiful jewelery, the horses leave the stables to join a procession to the Bada Chowk, the vast palace courtyard where, in days past, cavalries of elephants were shown on review. The Maharana awaits them solemnly; one after the other, he blesses his horses, following strict rules dictated by the Brahman of the royal family who sits beside him.

According to legend, the pedigree of the Marwari horses goes back to "the time when the horse had wings." Today, the Marwari horses, clearly identifiable by their inwardly curving ears, are threatened with extinction. But the House of Mewar is determined to maintain the breeding of these horses who still convey a mystical power. In an independent, democratic India, so passionately involved with modernity, at the Udaipur Palace stables, the House of Mewar ensures that the horses are honored, thus perpetuating a secular tradition from another age, but one that is still as powerful as ever.

Several times a year, the Marwari horses from the stables of the city palace put on their finery, decorated with silks and jewels. Halra, a many stranded silver necklace; kilingi, an ornament worn between their ears; neveri, a silver bracelet worn at the knee of some of these jewels; and dumachi.

A Mewars will say that without their horses they would never have survived; this is the origin of the love and respect they show in caring for the Marwari horses.

ROYAL STABLES FOR
THE HORSES OF THE DESERT

Amman, Jordan

One day Allah called the Wind of the South, took a handful of it and, throwing it on the ground, said: "I create you and I name you Arab." Thus, the Arab horse was born in the heart of the desert.

This legend is famous all over the world. But nowhere more than in Jordan is the everyday existence of horses endowed with such a palpable mythic dimension. When one admires the graceful silhouette of an Arab thoroughbred in the distance, the whole history of a people stands before one's eyes. The intelligent faces of these precious mounts express the entire tradition of a country rich in history and culture. In this original land, the mind is constantly drawn back to the past.

The Royal Jordan Stud Farm is a storybook of images and dreams. A mysterious attraction exerts a fascinating and poignant effect on those who stand before this temple to the Arab horse.

Is it because the roots of these dynasties lie deep in the founding myths of our cultures? For all its royal refinement, this stud farm is still inhabited primarily by the raw and wild lives of the Bedouins.

Is it because the horses bred here are descended from the most authentic thoroughbreds in the world?

Is it because the stud farm was created by a king whose descendants are still in power? Every member of the royal family is involved in breeding the horses, as if the horses were one of the attributes of their majesty.

The Royal Jordan Stud Farm is a surprising mixture that brings together the harshness of the desert and the cool of the stables, the austerity of a nomadic people and the inherited sophistication of the ancient Nabob civilization. The royal stables rise up at the edge of the desert, perched on a dry and rocky outcrop. Initially, the pious visitors who have come to pay their respects to this

Previous page: The Royal Stud of Jordan, painted in the colors of the Mediterranean, was created by King Abdullah Al Hussein for his Arab thoroughbreds, descendants of legendary horses.

Left: The serene peace of the evening on one of the three patios that are staggered down a hillside.

Next pages: The Arab horse is the reflection of a whole civilization. The royal Jordan family, headed by Princess Alia, is well aware of this; she gives her horses a shelter worthy of this honor.

equine temple of Arabian horses, focus on long horizontal lines cutting across the building, interrupted by courtyards and fountains.

Three square courtyards are interconnected, leading from one to the next, with a fountain in the center. A thin rivulet of water trickles down from a pedestal decorated with blue mosaics. The cool white of the stalls is brightened by ceramic tiles that are turquoise, lapis-lazuli, and celadon, as colorful as precious stones. The water mirrors the sky and an infinite calm gently lulls the air. Water is the source of life: all around the fountains, in the early morning the stables awaken to the world. One by one the horses leave their stalls and walk nonchalantly through the inner arcades of the courtyard to quench their thirst at the fountains. In the summer they are given a refreshing shower to help them face the crushing heat of the day.

The horses of the Royal Jordan Stables are very imaginative: if you listen closely, below the splashing of the water, you will hear them telling tales.

Baz, the great, great grandson of Noah, was the first to tame the mare Kehilet. This legendary line is apparently the origin of the rare, authentic, Arab thoroughbreds, whose descendants now gather round the cool water of the fountains in the stud farm.

Another legend tells that after his marriage to the Queen of Sheba, Solomon welcomed a caravan of Bedouins to his palace. Before returning to the desert, the travelers requested gifts to help them continue on their journey. Solomon gave them a horse, with the words: "Here are your provisions: when you are hungry, one of your men will go hunting on this steed. Hardly will you have time to light a fire before he will return with game." The Bedouins reached their destination safe and sound.

Noah, Baz, Solomon . . . all these mythic references remind us that the people of the Bible were all nomadic or semi-nomadic. Their way of life forced them to take good care of their horses, for their survival depended on them. These were the nomads who wandered over the area now known as Jordan.

In more recent times, the deeds of the small horses that accompanied the Arab warriors allied to the English troops led by Lawrence of Arabia are still famous in Amman. King Abdullah Al Hussein created the stud farm for them. Since the mid-1960s, the Royal Stables have housed the stallions and mares of its elite troop, allowing them to found a dynasty of their own blood. The Royal Jordan Stud Farm stables are proof of the loyal passion that links the Arab people to their mounts: it is the grateful homeland paying its respects to its brave companions.

The myth must not die: this is the wish of the Royal Jordan Stud Farm. Princess Alia Al Hussein, the sister of King Abdullah II, today heads the Royal Stud Farm and has taken over the breeding. Rich in unique lineage, Jordan is once again among the greatest countries breeding Arab thoroughbreds.

As a symbol of royal power, a place that conserves a wild world and concentrates on the breeding of unusual horses, the Royal Jordan Stud Farm has managed to take hold of its history and use it as a fertile base. For many years to come the inheritors of the legendary horses will find peace there, so long as the water flows in the fountains.

On each patio, a fountain creates an oasis effect. The Royal Stud sits on the edge of the town, where the desert begins.

*Horses are the messengers of furusiya, the
medieval art of war on horseback. Even
today, furusiya fascinates those interested
in horses and history.*

THE ROYAL ANDALUSIAN SCHOOL
OF EQUESTRIAN ART

Jerez de la Frontera, Spain

At the heart of beautiful Jerez, the jewel of Andalusia stands proud in a verdant setting. This is where the best mounts and horsemen of the haute école live and work. Jerez is the dream of a horseman who, in this magical setting, created one of the most prestigious schools for equestrian arts in the world, a symbol of excellence for the dressage of Spanish thoroughbreds. Elegant buildings, worthy of this highly prestigious art, express the determined passion of founder Don Alvaro Domecq Romero, an expert rider and horse enthusiast.

Behind the monumental portal of the Royal Andalusian School of Equestrian Art hides the Duke d'Abrantes' Palace, designed by French architect Charles Garnier. This phenomenal four-floor building is comparable to the most beautiful neoclassical monuments. Nothing suggests that less than thirty years ago the site was derelict. Today the Recreo Palace is clean, tidy, and orderly, as if it had remained intact since when it was first built.

Struck by an impression of vastness in the great park lying before them, visitors discover the imposing central building, painted in typical Spanish colors: immaculate white with saffron yellow edges. Gradually, as they become more familiar with the view, other details begin to emerge: the stable top towers, bull's-eye windows, and blue and white tiling.

Finally, visitors notice the movement of the horses. They are training, reigns held tight as they practice the classical figures of haute école. One paws the ground while another works out a capriole. Suddenly visitors are right back in the seventeenth century, when the dressage of Andalusian horses was one of the defining privileges of European nobility. As a symbol of power and might, discipline was raised to the level of pure art.

The texts and paintings from riding schools in the classic era inspired Domecq to create a spectacle that involved countless hours of work: "How the Andalusian

Previous pages: The walls of the great riding arena are punctuated with round windows, all around the stables and technical facilities, such as the veterinary unit. Every morning the horses and riders go through this door to train in the shadow of the trees that protect the arena (page 172).

Left: The inner courtyard where the horses are saddled. After daily training sessions or shows, the saddles and harnesses are cleaned.

Below: An installation for caring for the horses.

The vast glass roof of the inside riding arena
filters the dazzling rays of the Andalusian sun,
allowing through only a gentle, warm light.
It is time to prepare the horses for the show.
Soon they will enter the arena ready to impress
thousands of spectators with their skills.

After the show, the calm returns to the four wings of the stallion stable. The last job is to sweep the paving and wash the floor with water to freshen and cool the air. The bull's-eye windows at the end of each wing echo those in the main riding arena.

No tack room is as impressive as the one in the
Royal Andalusian School of Jerez. The wooden
panels exude a unique aroma. On three floors,
above the gallery, precious harnesses and
beautiful saddles are displayed behind
windows. Below are the facilities for everyday
use. In the middle of the room, a giant palm
tree ensures that the leather does not dry out by
maintaining a sufficiently humid atmosphere.

182

Horses Dance." The first shows took place at Los Alburejos.

Domecq wanted to show his respect for his noble country's tradition. Convinced that he should pursue his project to found a school and present the academic exercises of Spanish thoroughbred horses and their exceptional riding masters, he looked for a suitably prestigious setting. In 1975, his dream became a reality when the Department of Information and Tourism, which had been supporting the school for several years already, bought the Recreo Palace, formerly the Duke of Abrantes' estate. This derelict estate quickly turn into one of the most prestigious equestrian school in the world.

The existing buildings have been restored in the purest Andalusian style. For public spectacles, in 1980 a riding ring with 1,600 seats, including a royal box, was built; the new stables could house about sixty horses. Everything was designed with meticulous respect for the slightest detail:

the training grounds, work areas, air-conditioned saddle rooms that prevent the leather from drying out, a clinic with an operating room for caring for the mounts.

The prestige of the establishment was indisputable. Twelve years after its creation, His Majesty the King of Spain conferred the title of "Royal School" on the institution and accepted the post of honorary president. On October 15 of the same year, King Juan Carlos and Queen Sofia presided over the inaugural event. In July 2003, the Royal School became a foundation supported by the Ministry of Trade, Tourism and Sports of the Andalusian Government, allowing it to receive private funds. Every year 200,000 visitors come to see the show at Jerez, "How the Andalusian Horses Dance." The Royal School has given future generations, both horses and riders, the tools for achieving excellence. They will continue to excel, without flinching, for years to come, to the delight of their admirers.

184

The Palace of the Duke d'Abrantes, built by French architect Charles Garnier, has a magnificent tower, and a roof decorated with a bull's-eye window. This round window is found on all the new buildings, providing a guiding thread throughout the architecture of the riding school.

GAZETEER

DIRECTORY OF STABLES

ACKNOWLEDGMENTS

Jean-Louis Gouraud, Joël Farges, Yves Bruezière, Arnaud Guilbert, Thomas Lépine,
Catherine Bonifassi and her staff, Philippe Feinsilber, Anne-Laure Madec, Hanka and Rémy Prud'homme,
Françoise and Benoît Vayron de la Moureyre, Agnès and Jean-François de Bénazé,
Decia de Pauw, Baudouin Allais, Alia Al Hussein, Ghalia Nooredin, Gérard Gémin, Joe Osborne,
Tom Gallagher, Cristobal Egerström, Federica Zanco, Lord Palmer, Bill, Count Federico Zichy Thyssen,
Maharana Arvind Singh, Princess Bhargavi Mewar, Sabina Bailey, Antoine Poupel, Chiaki Makiura,
Takamasa Inaba, Kip Mistral, Basha O'Reilly, Guy de Rothshild, the Wertimer brothers,
Charles Miers, Agnès Galletier, Tanja Münster, Chantal Desmazière, Anne Zweibaum,
Klaus Kirschbaum, Sophie Praquin, Christine Marchandise and Carolyn Shread.

This book is inspired by a series of documentaries entitled
Ecuries Extraordinaires, produced by Kolam Production: films@kolam.fr

CREDITS

THIS BOOK HAS BEEN CREATED BY

\\ EDITORIAL CONCEPTION \\ REDACTION
CATHERINE BONIFASSI
with:
ANSWERS COMMUNICATION
CLAIRE ARJAKOVSKY
GENEVIÈVE BÉGOU
VANESSA BLONDEL
JEAN-PIERRE COLIGNON
DAPHNÉ COUSINEAU
PHILIPPE FEINSILBER
MURIEL GIRAUD
ANNE-LAURE MADEC
FRANCINE SIRVEN

\\ DESIGN
PATRICE RENARD
with:
JULIE BORDES
JULIEN GUILLEMARD
JIMMY PINA

\\ PHOTOENGRAVING
GCS
LC PHOTOGRAVURE

First published in the United States of America in 2006 by
Rizzoli International Publications, Inc.
300 Park Avenue South
New York, NY 10010
www.rizzoliusa.com

Originally created in French as *Ecuries Extraordinaires* in 2006 by
CASSI EDITION
2, cité Dupetit Thouars
75003 Paris

Second printing, 2006
2006 2007 2008 / 10 9 8 7 6 5 4 3 2

ISBN-10: 0-8478-2815-8
ISBN-13: 978-0-8478-2815-9

Library of Congress Control Number: 2006922007

Printed in Spain